Published by Scarab Hill Publishing
Sutton, Surrey

ISBN 978-1-9161330-0-6

This book was written by Angela Mohun
and designed by Beverly Jones.

Contents

Unité 1
Dans mon sac

Learning to:
Name my school equipment

Dans mon sac

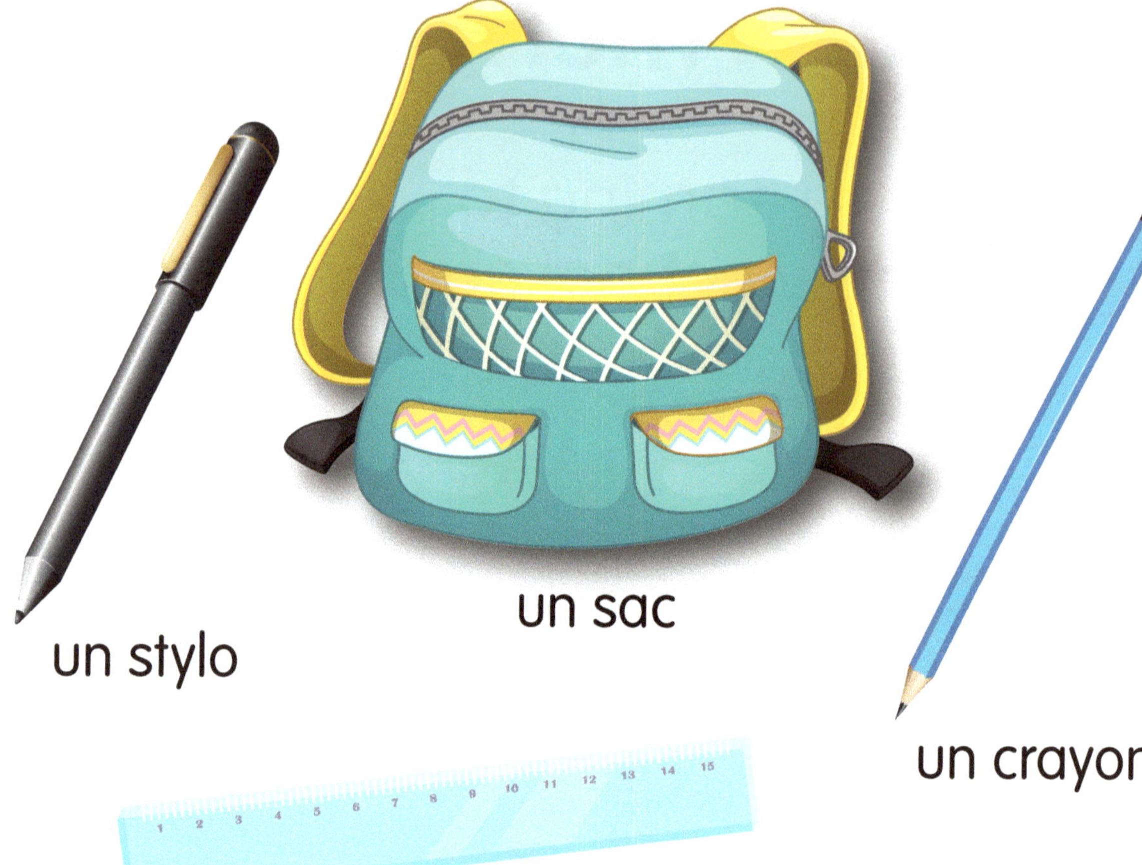

un sac

un stylo

un crayon

un règle

un taille-crayon

une calculatrice

une gomme

des ciseaux

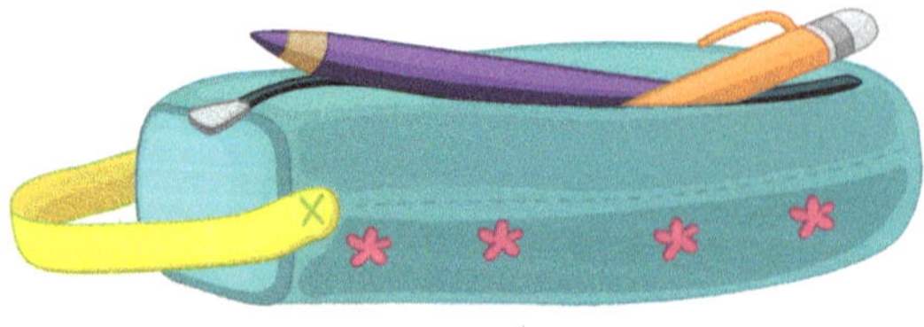

une trousse

Complete the words

une _ _ _ _ _

des ci _ _ _ _ _

une calcula _ _ _ _ _

un st _ _ _

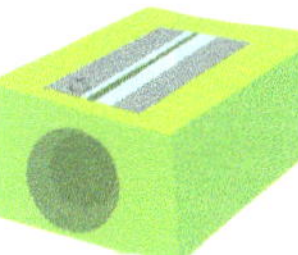

un taille- _ _ _ _ _ _ _

un cr _ _ _ _ _

un r _ _ _ _ _

une _ _ _ _ _ _ _ _

un _ _ _

 © 2019 J'adore le français by Angela Mohun

Match the words
to the pictures

un **crayon**

une **règle**

un **sac**

un **stylo**

des **ciseaux**

une **trousse**

un **taille-crayon**

une **gomme**

une **calculatrice**

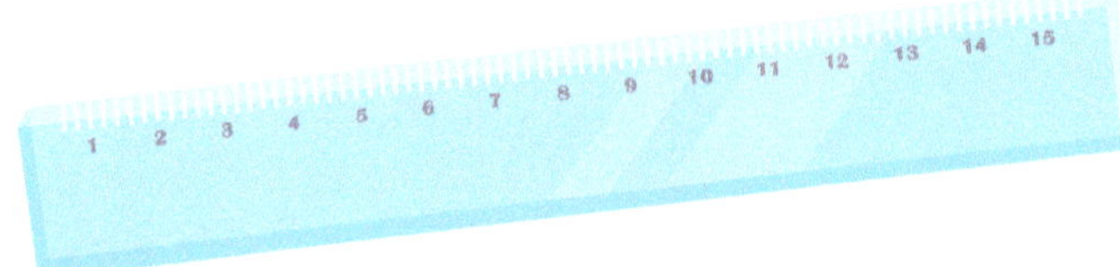

Make a short sentence using J'ai

J'ai = I have

Complete the sentences following the examples

J'ai un stylo

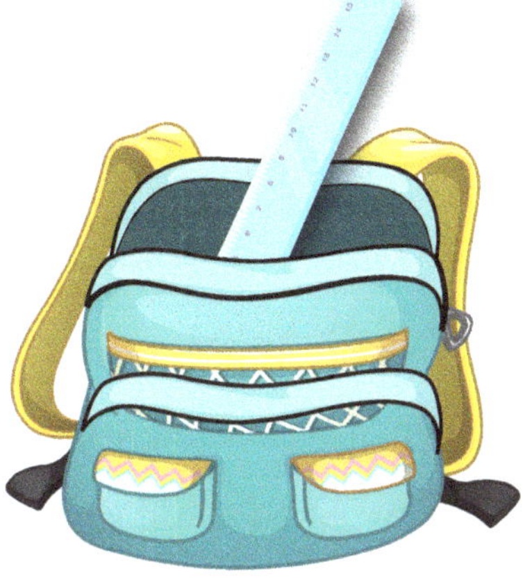

J'ai une règle

J'ai ______________

J'ai ______________

J'ai ______________

J'ai ______________

J'ai ______________

et = and

J'ai __________ et ____________

  © 2019 J'adore le français by Angela Mohun

Draw what you have in your bag and create your own sentence on the dotted line

....

....

....

....

Felt tips = Des feutres
A compass = Un compas
Coloured pencils = Des crayons de couleur
a reading book = Un livre
An excercise book = Un cahier

 © 2019 J'adore le français by Angela Mohun

Test de vocabulaire

Dans mon sac = In my bag
J'ai = I have
Je n'ai pas de = I don't have a

Using the word bank, match the English words to the French words

WORD BANK
a bag • a rubber • a pencil sharpener • a calculator
scissors • a pencil case • a pencil • a pen

Un crayon ....

Une règle ....

Un sac ....

Un stylo ....

Des ciseaux ....

Une trousse ....

Un taille-crayon ....

Une gomme ....

Une calculatrice ....

Point Grammaire
Un is followed by a masculine noun
Une is followed by a feminine noun

Challenge yourself

Point Grammaire
The negative form
Je n'ai pas de = I don't have a

How to form the negative in French 

J'ai un sac — I have a bag

 Je n'ai pas un sac

 Je n'ai pas de sac

I do not have a bag

Challenge yourself

Practice
The negative form
Je **n'ai pas de** = I don't have a

Je **n'ai pas de** sac

Je n'ai pas de ....

....

....

....

Create your own sentence

....

Tick the correct negative sentences

1. ☐ **Je n'ai pas de stylo.**
2. ☐ Je n'ai de crayon.
3. ☐ Je n'ai pas une gomme.
4. ☐ Je n'ai règle.
5. ☐ Je n'ai pas de sac.
6. ☐ Je n'ai trousse.
7. ☐ Je n'ai pas de ciseaux.
8. ☐ Je n'ai pas taille-crayon.
9. ☐ Je n'ai pas de calculatrice.

Extension
Rewrite the wrong sentences correctly

____

____

____

Practise the following sentences with a friend

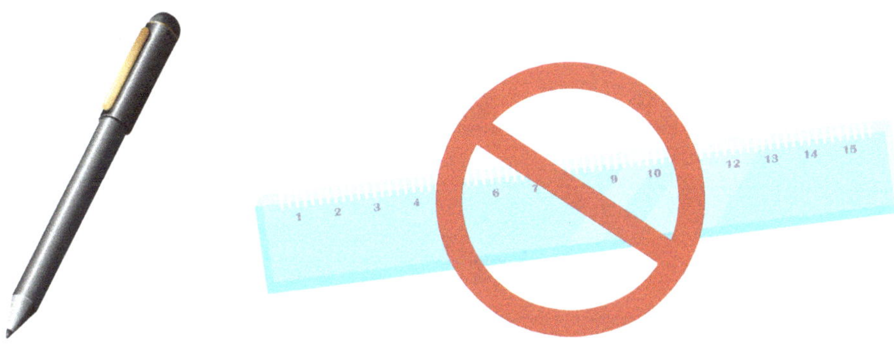

J'ai un/une …
Je n'ai pas de …

Extension

Spot the missing sentence and write it below using j'ai or je n'ai pas de or both!

____

____

____

Label the pictures

WORD BANK
des ciseaux • une gomme • un taille-crayon•
une règle • une trousse • une calculatrice

J'ai = I have
Je **n'ai** **pas de** = I don't have a

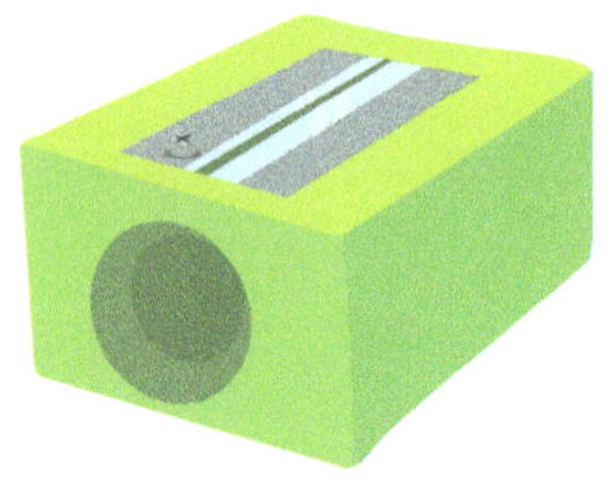

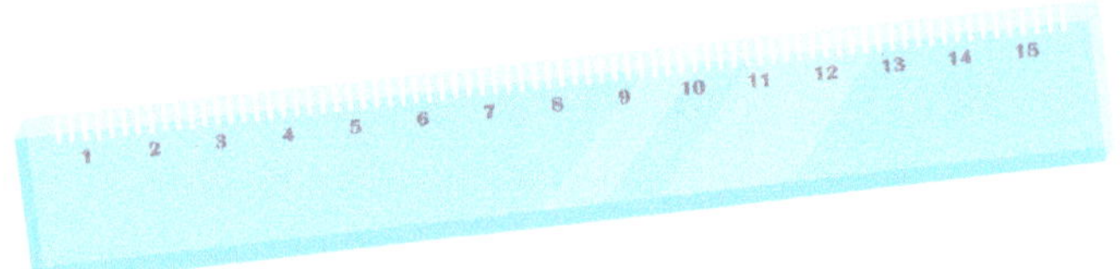

....

....

....

END OF UNIT ASSESSMENT
CAN I ...

☐ **Remember at least three items?**

☐ **Make full sentences?**

☐ **Make full negative sentences?**

Unité 2
Mon visage et mon corps

Learning to:
Name and describe my facial features
Name and describe parts of my body

Mon visage

la tête

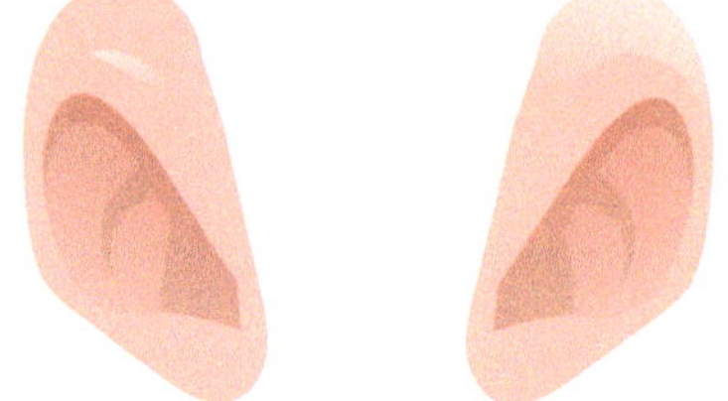

les yeux

les oreilles

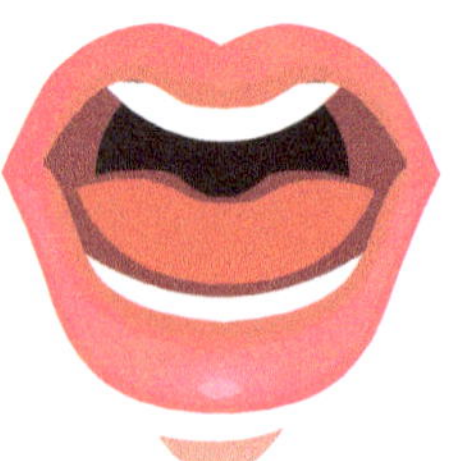

la bouche

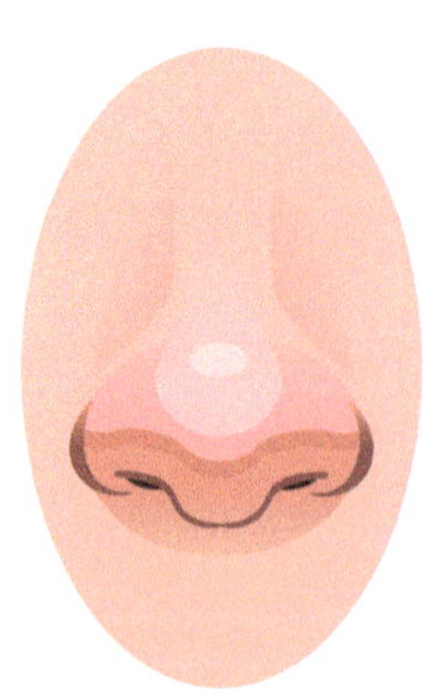

le nez

les cheveux

Label the pictures

WORD BANK
les cheveux • la bouche • le nez
les oreilles • la tête • les yeux

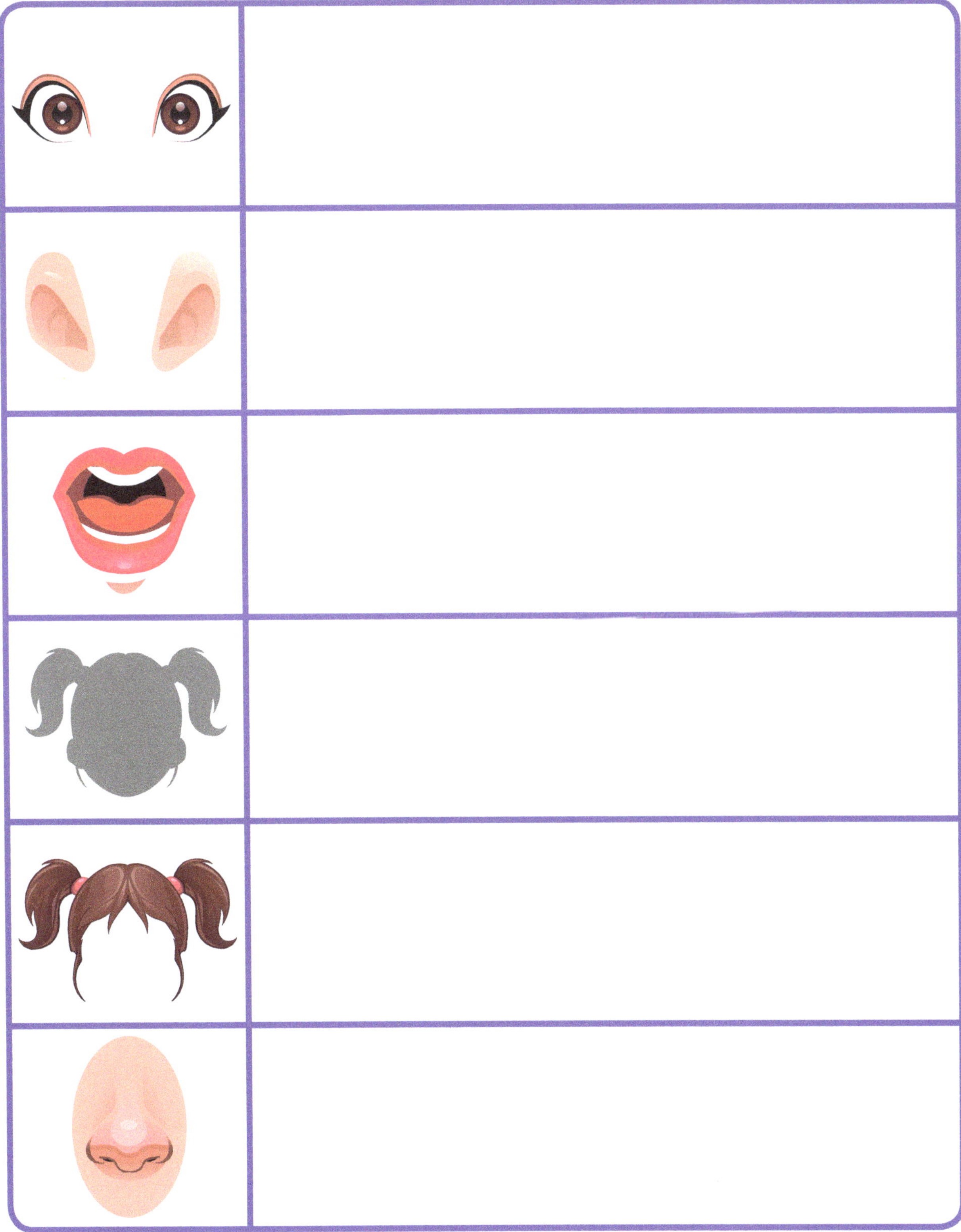

Label the picture using the word bank

WORD BANK
les cheveux • la bouche • le nez
les oreilles • la tête • les yeux

© 2019 J'adore le français by Angela Mohun

Draw your self portrait and label it in French

EXTRA VOCABULARY
cheeks = les joues   the forehead = le front
eyebrows = les sourcils   teeth = les dents
lips = les lèvres

Mon corps

les épaules

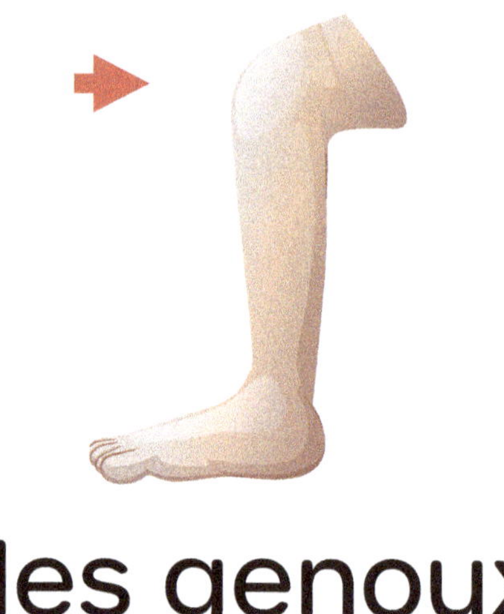

les genoux

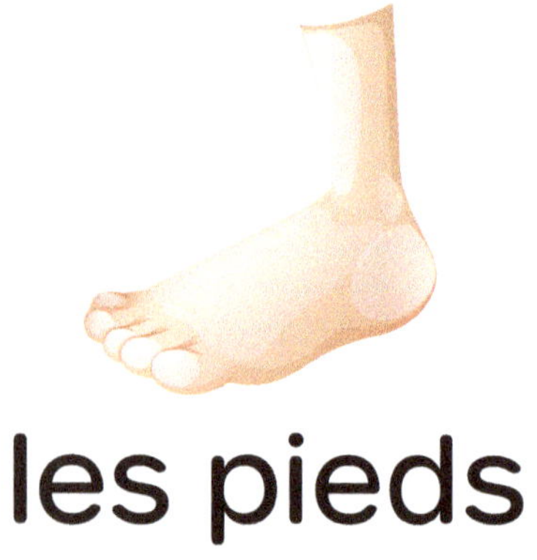

les pieds

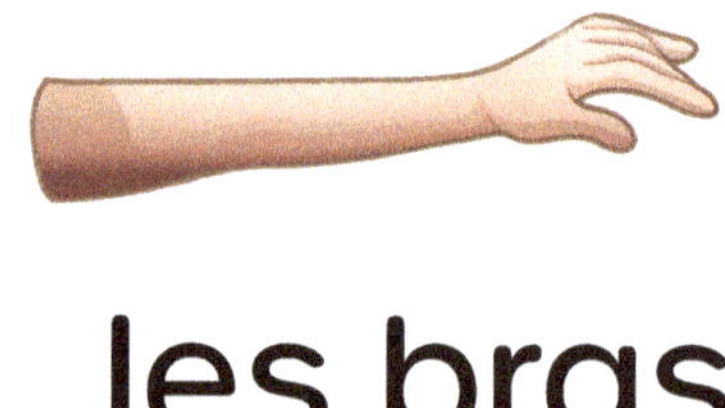

les bras

la main

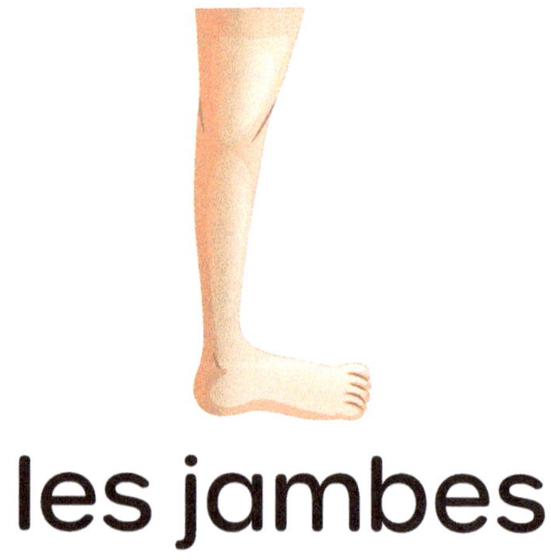

les jambes

Mon monstre

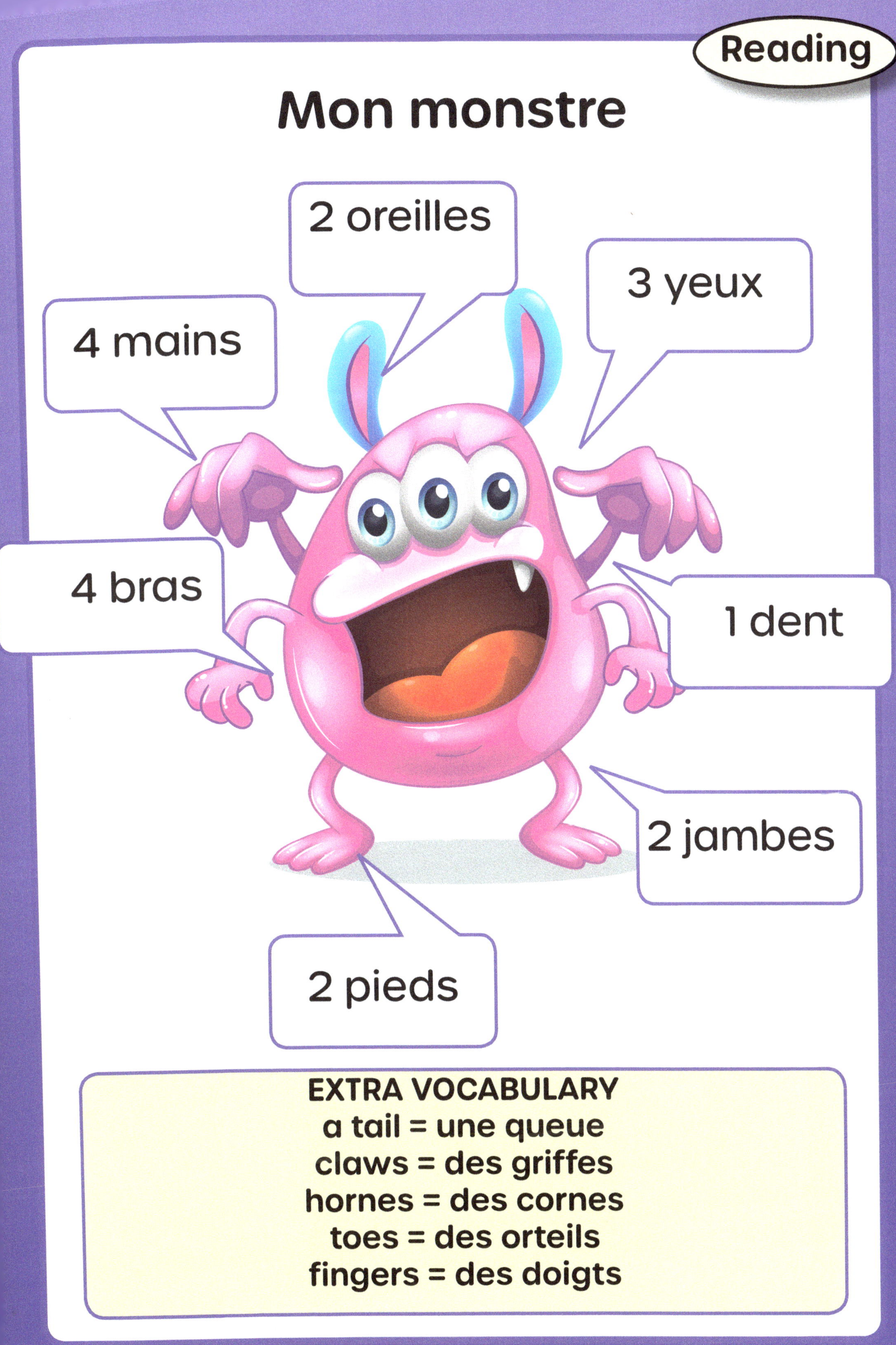

EXTRA VOCABULARY
a tail = une queue
claws = des griffes
hornes = des cornes
toes = des orteils
fingers = des doigts

Mon monstre
Draw your own horrible monster and label it in French.

Mots-mélés
Le visage et le corps

Z	C	E	O	H	M	H	O	O	F	W	S	L	T	O
X	U	A	V	S	E	B	M	A	J	S	E	L	D	I
E	G	I	V	R	W	G	W	L	F	S	L	A	N	J
E	N	L	G	S	L	C	D	X	C	E	L	T	Z	R
G	I	N	Y	Y	R	H	I	H	S	L	I	Ê	A	E
A	S	M	G	T	Y	R	E	G	S	U	E	T	L	D
H	M	R	P	K	V	V	E	A	U	A	R	E	E	I
L	A	H	T	Z	E	N	R	D	Z	P	O	T	C	Q
E	E	H	C	U	O	B	A	L	N	É	S	M	E	A
Z	M	H	X	U	S	D	E	I	P	S	E	L	W	U
X	E	C	X	E	I	S	A	C	F	E	L	W	I	E
A	Q	N	L	V	Y	M	Q	S	G	L	U	I	G	D
B	D	F	E	E	A	L	U	G	H	E	V	Q	X	E
O	S	D	U	L	J	W	J	R	L	M	A	N	T	K
F	J	X	D	S	G	Q	M	O	E	N	F	O	Y	K

LA BOUCHE   LES ÉPAULES

LE NEZ   LES GENOUX

LES OREILLES   LES PIEDS

LES YEUX   LES BRAS

LES CHEVEUX   LA MAIN

LA TÊTE   LES JAMBES

Unité 3
Décrire mon visage

Learning to:
Describe myself physically
using colours

Les couleurs

Rouge - Red

Jaune - Yellow

Bleu - Blue

Vert - Green

Orange

Violet - Purple

Rose - Pink

Marron - Brown

Gris - Grey

Noir - Black

Blanc - White

Les couleurs

Point Grammaire

Colours and other adjectives are placed **after** the noun The *black* cat = Le chat *noir*

Write the colour you see in the pictures in French

Un chien *blanc*

Une pomme ___________

Un hibou ___________

Une banane ___________

Une baleine ___________

Un requin ___________

Un cochon ___________

Un serpent ___________

Un chat ___________

Describing using colours
Complete the sentences

 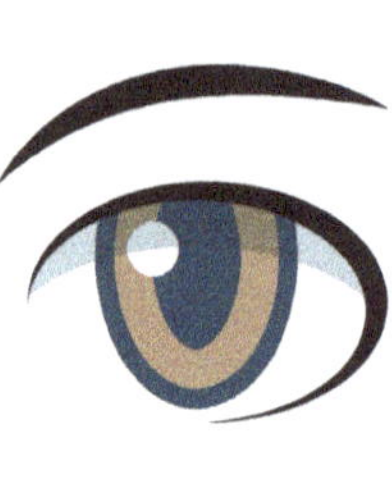

Les yeux noisette

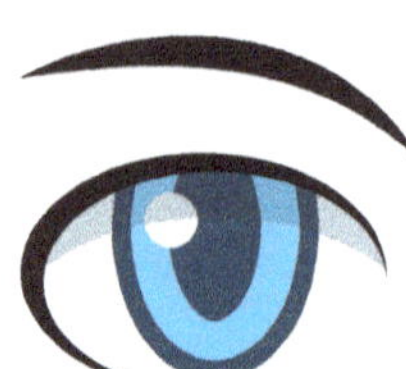 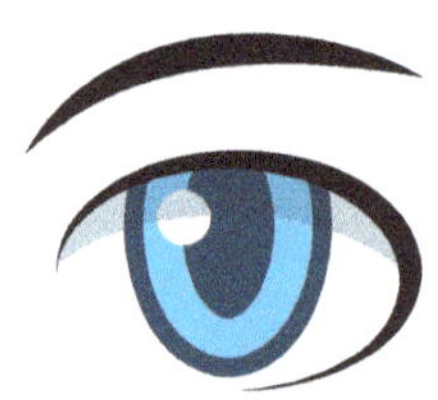

Les yeux _ _ _ _ _

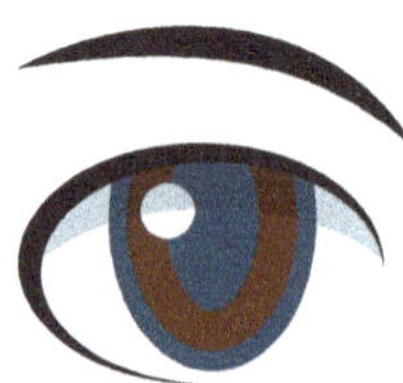 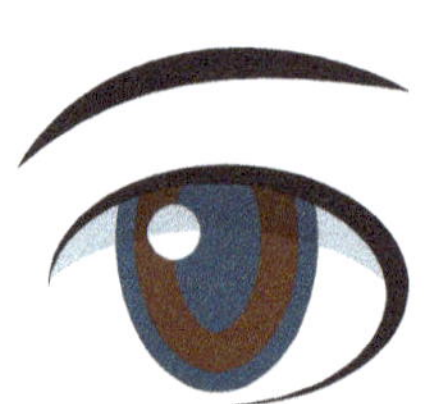

Les yeux _ _ _ _ _ _ _ _

 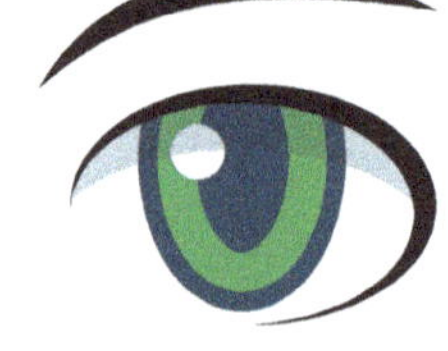

_ _ _ _ _ _ _ verts

Les cheveux noirs   Les _ _ _ _ _ _ _ _ blonds   Les cheveux _ _ _ _ _

Les cheveux _ _ _ _ _   Les _ _ _ _ _ _ _ _ roux

Point Grammaire

J'ai = I have
Brown hair = Cheveux bruns
Ginger hair = Cheveux roux

1. Who has brown hair? ________________________

2. Who has red hair? ________________________

3. Who has hazel eyes? ________________________

Colour in the pictures using the right colours

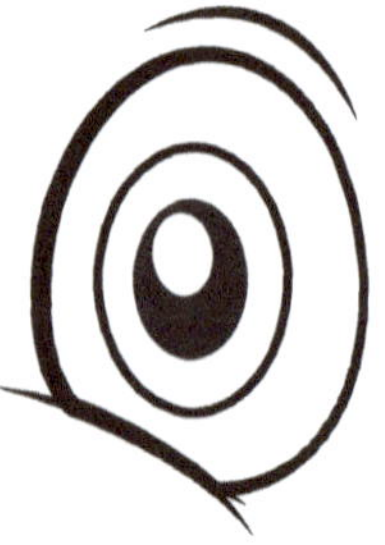 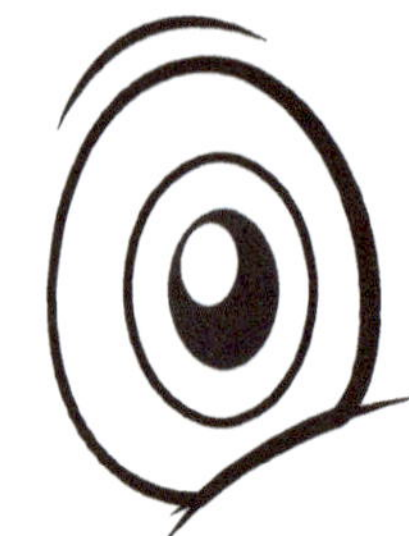

J'ai les yeux bleus

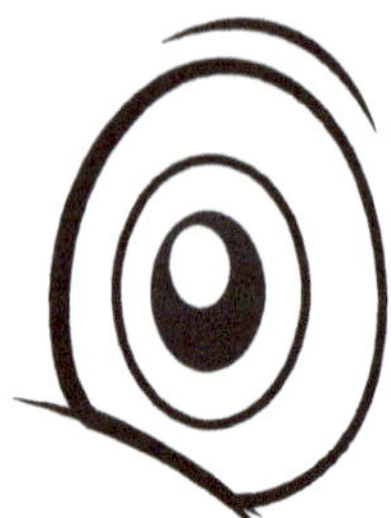 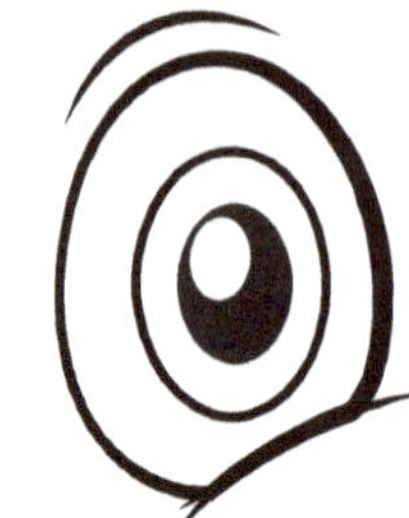

J'ai les yeux verts

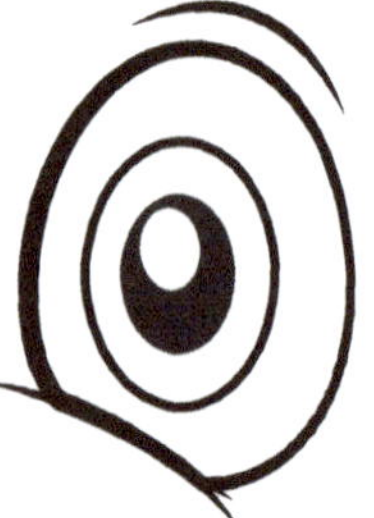 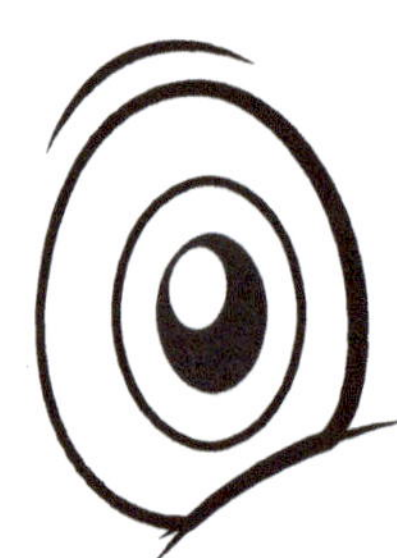

J'ai les yeux marron

 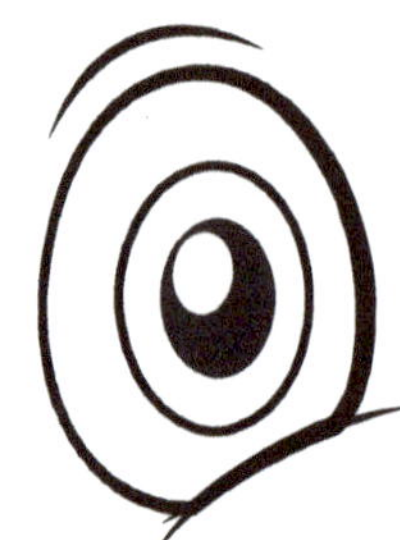

J'ai les yeux noisette

J'ai les cheveux

blonds   gris   noirs

roux   bruns

Mon auto-portrait

Draw a picture of yourself and complete the speech bubble in French

Je m'appelle _______________________

J'ai les yeux _______________________

et j'ai les cheveux _______________________

END OF UNIT ASSESSMENT
CAN I ...

- ☐ Remember at least three face or body parts?

- ☐ Start making short sentences?

- ☐ Make full sentences using J'ai?

What I liked most was...

The most challenging was...

Unité 4
Les animaux domestiques

Learning to:
Name and describe pets

Les animaux

un chat

un oiseau

un chien

un poisson

un hamster

une araignée

un lapin

un serpent

Match the picture to the label, by drawing a line.

un oiseau

un chat

un poisson

une araignée

un chien

un hamster

un lapin

un serpent

Circle the correct answer

un chat

un chien

un hamster

un lapin

un oiseau

un poisson

une araignée

un serpent

Point Grammaire

Colours and other adjectives are placed after the noun
a **red** bird = un oiseau **rouge**

Rouge   Jaune   Bleu   Vert   Orange   Violet

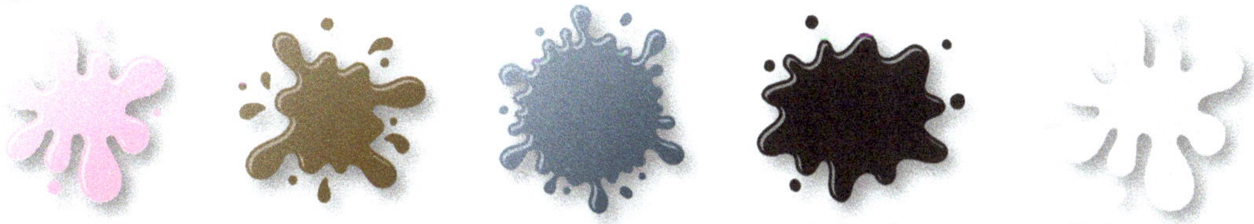

Rose   Marron   Gris   Noir   Blanc

Un oiseau jaune    Un oiseau rouge    Un oiseau bleu

Colour the bird with the right colour

Un oiseau vert   Un oiseau rose   Un oiseau marron

Complete the sentences

Un lapin
blanc

Un serpent

____

Un hamster

____

Un chat

____

Un poisson

____

Un chien

____

Une araignée

____

Un oiseau

____

Draw and colour an
animal and label it in French

 © 2019 J'adore le français by Angela Mohun

Label the picture and colour the animals with a colour of your choice

Une araignée **noire**

____

____

____

____

____

____

____

Challenge yourself

Point Grammaire
The negative form
Je **n'ai pas de** = I don't have a

How to form the negative in French 

J'ai un chat I have a cat

 **Je n'ai pas un chat**

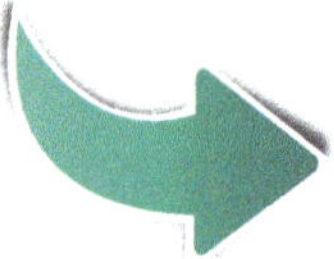 **Je n'ai pas de chat**

I do not have a cat

Extension
change the colours in a new sentence

Challenge yourself

Write the sentence according to the pictures

 J'ai un chat gris

 Je n'ai pas de chat gris

____

____

____

____

____

Draw your pet and write your own sentence

____

____

____

____

END OF UNIT ASSESSMENT
CAN I ...

☐ **Remember two animals?**

☐ **Describe my pet using colours?**

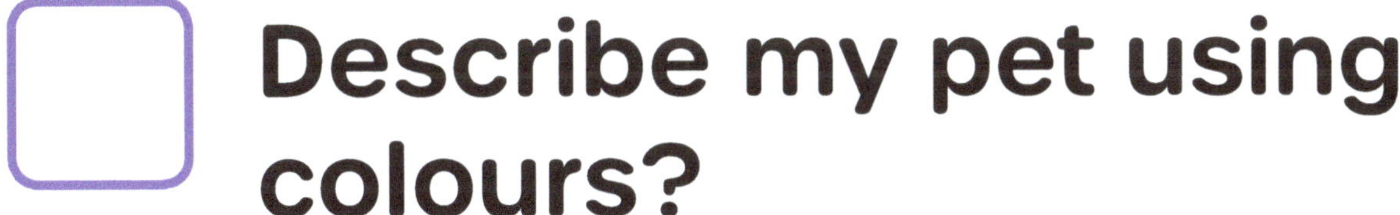

☐ **Make sentences using J'ai and Je n'ai pas de?**

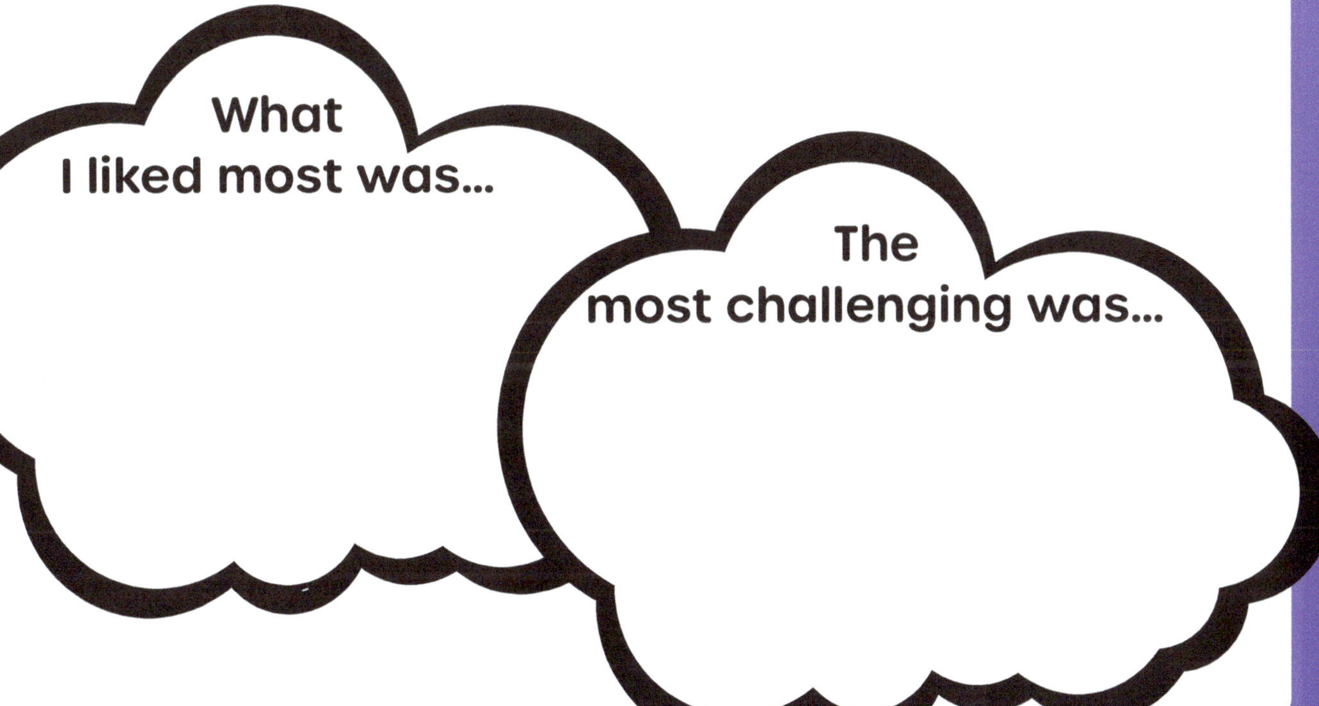

 © 2019 J'adore le français by Angela Mohun

Unité 5
Les sports

Learning to:
Name sports and
expressing likes and dislikes

Can you match the sports with the pictures

1. **Le** skateboard
2. **La** natation
3. **La** gymnastique
4. **La** danse
5. **L'**athlétisme
6. **Le** foot
7. **Le** basketball
8. **Le** badminton
9. **Le** tennis
10. **Le** cyclisme

Opinions

J'aime
I like

Je n'aime pas
I dislike

J'aime le foot
I like football

Je n'aime pas l'athlétisme
I don't like athletics

1. In the boxes below draw a sport you like and one you dislike
2. Complete the sentences

J'aime ___________   Je n'aime pas ______

 © 2019 J'adore le français by Angela Mohun

Opinions

J'adore
I really like/ I love

Je déteste
I hate

J'adore la danse
I love dance

Je déteste le tennis
I hate tennis

1. In the boxes below draw a sport you love and one you hate
2. Complete the sentences

J'adore _____________   Je déteste_____________

  © 2019 J'adore le français by Angela Mohun

Point Grammaire

I like tennis = J'aime le tennis
In French we add the articles 'le' or 'la' before the sport

Tick if the sentences are correct:

1. ☐ J'aime le cyclisme
2. ☐ Je n'aime pas badminton
3. ☐ Je déteste le foot
4. ☐ J'aime le skateboard
5. ☐ J'adore danse
6. ☐ Je déteste natation
7. ☐ Je n'aime pas la gymnastique

Extension

Rewrite the wrong sentences correctly.

____

____

____

____

Practise the following sentences with a friend

 J'aime

 Je n'aime pas

J'adore

 J'adore

 Je déteste

Challenge yourself
Translate the following sentences into English

1. J'aime le basket   I like basketball

2. J'adore le badminton _______________

3. Je n'aime pas le skate_______________

4. Je déteste le tennis _______________

5. J'adore la natation _______________

6. I like tennis_______________________

7. I love basketball _______________

Extension
Complete the sentences

1. J'adore _______________________________

2. _______________________________ le cricket.

3. _______________________________ le ski.

4. Je déteste _______________________________

END OF UNIT ASSESSMENT
CAN I ...

☐ **Remember at least four sports?**

☐ **Say what sport I like?**

☐ **Say what sport I dislike?**

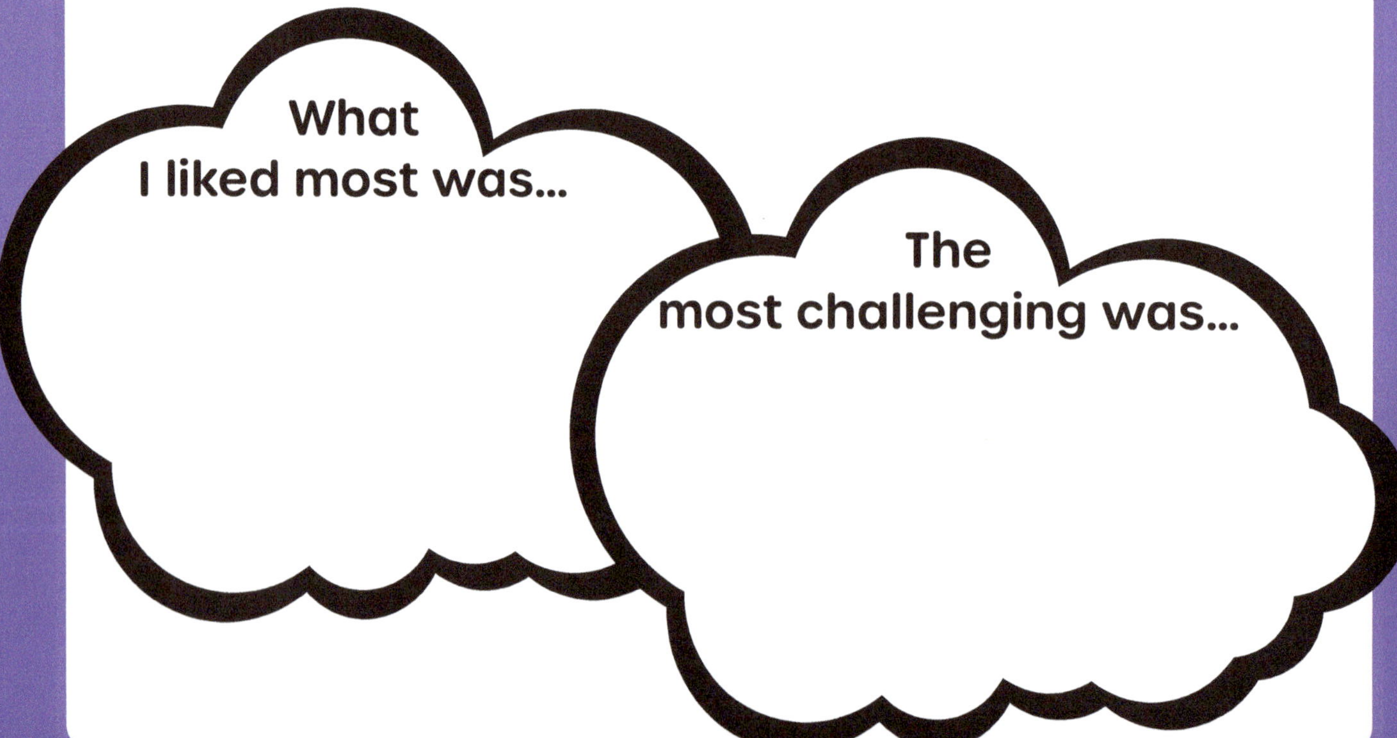

Unité 6
Les vêtements

Learning to:
Say what you wear for sports

Pour le sport

Un short

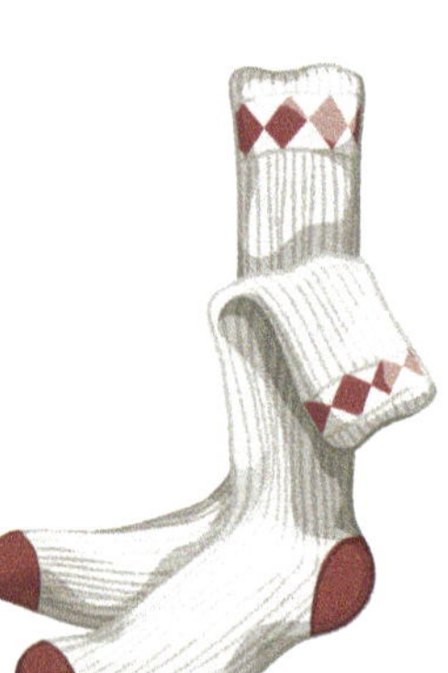

Des chaussettes

Un tee-shirt

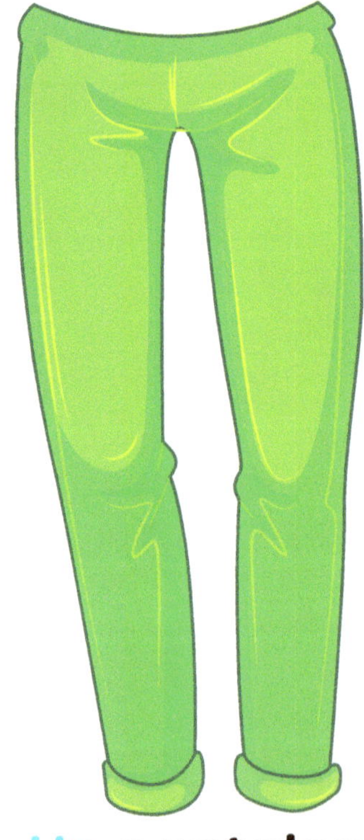

Un pantalon

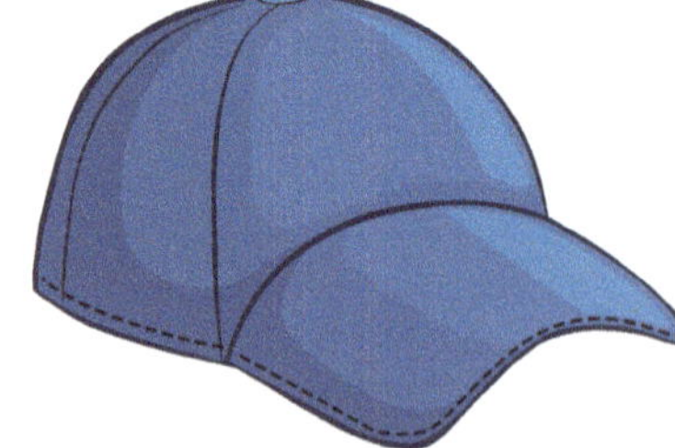

Une casquette

Un maillot de bain

Une jupe

Des baskets

Pour le tennis

Pour la natation

Label the pictures following the examples above:

 © 2019 J'adore le français by Angela Mohun

Pour le sport = For sport
Je porte = I wear
et = and

Complete the speech bubbles

Ce que je porte

Draw yourself playing your favourite sport and complete the speech bubble using 'je porte':

Solve the crossword puzzle:
***Write the French words using the clues below.**

* Write in 'un, une, des'. Leave no gaps.

Across	Down
4. a skirt	1. trainers
6. shorts	2. a cap
7. a swimsuit	3. socks
	4. trousers
	5. a t-shirt

END OF UNIT ASSESSMENT
CAN I ...

- [ ] remember at least two pieces of clothing.

- [ ] name clothing for a specific sport.

- [ ] say what you wear using 'Je porte'.

 © 2019 J'adore le français by Angela Mohun